SEE OF

CHAN GES SHARING GREAT
OM FOR A BETTER LIFE

ADRIENNE GREEN

Seeds Of Hope

First edition printed and published in the United Kingdom 2024.

A CIP catalogue record of this book is available from the British Library.

ISBN: 978-1-7384734-6-5 (Paperback)
ISBN 978-1-7384734-7-2 (eBook)
Imprint: Independently published
Cover design: Jenn Garside Illustration and Graphic Design
Typesetting: Matthew J Bird

For further information about this book, please contact the author: www.adriennegreen.co.uk

Dedication

To my beloved Mel, whose unwavering patience and profound understanding sustained me throughout the creation of this book. In countless moments beside sacred trees and ancient stone circles he intuitively guarded the sanctity of our communion, ensuring my connection remained undisturbed.

Contents

FOREWORD

Step into the enchanting world of mindfulness and explore the spiritual essence of trees with a captivating new book by Adrienne Green. Having known Adrienne for several years and witnessed her dedication to holistic and spiritual well-being, I am thrilled to have been asked to introduce this pocket-sized gem which beckons readers to reconnect with themselves and nature.

In this "channelled book", Adrienne invites us to pause and reflect on the profound wisdom embodied by trees, nature and spirituality. Drawing inspiration from the ancient practise of forest bathing, amongst many things, this book gracefully .encourages us to immerse ourselves in the therapeutic embrace of nature. This book will help readers to discover the transformative power of being present in the company of these ancient sentient beings.

Perhaps they have a secret message of guidance for us, if we just become still in their presence?

A poignant quote, whose author remains a mystery, beautifully captures the essence of this book:

"Biologists affirm that trees are social beings. They count, learn, and remember. They nurture sick members, signal danger through an intricate fungal network, and sustain the ancient stumps of long- felled companions for centuries by nurturing them with sweet elixir through their roots."

Trees have been revered for centuries for reasons that are deeply rooted in ancient cultures, we have much to learn!

Adrienne beckons you to carry this pocket companion, as a reminder to cherish the profound lessons whispered by the leaves and the ancient echoes of the forest. A timeless invitation to reconnect with the heartbeats of nature.

Patrick Gamble

PREFACE

It is funny how when we reflect on life certain things become apparent.

If you'd asked me ten years ago about writing a book, I would have said, that's such a cliché that we all have a book inside of us, there's not a book inside me, just waiting to get out.

And yet, here I am, having nurtured a tiny seedling and allowed it to flourish into this book.

When I was in Glastonbury in the United Kingdom, completing my Reiki Master Teacher training, we visited the Chalice Wells, a special place of spiritual and healing energy. As we wandered around, I instinctively held back from the group and touched a tree. I had no idea what I was doing but I simply followed my internal intuition to do it. Then, to my surprise, as I stood there quietly, the tree spoke! Not a big, booming external voice, but a deep inner knowing almost like a whisper.

What did it say?

To me it said, 'I speak with your Walnut Tree'. In that instant, everything made sense. Although I lived in Norfolk, in the United Kingdom, both of these trees had roots in the same pot – the earth.

And that's where my journey began, or so I thought. While turning out some old photos, I came across one of me, aged three or four, clearly fascinated by a rubber tree in Singapore. So, this deep connection had remained hidden by the noise of modern-day life, just waiting for the right time to surface, when I would be still enough to hear.

Another nudge came along as I visited Southwest Scotland many years later and connected to an ancient Beech Tree (there is more about this encounter in the book). She taught me that we didn't have to be touching a tree to communicate, and that we can telepathically connect to their spirit and energy, just as we would a human.

And now, of course, they all talk or whisper to me. From my Walnut Tree, whom I thank out loud for all the walnuts I harvest each Autumn, to the trees I encounter on a walk in the local woods. They told me to move my bistro table and chairs underneath the Walnut tree and write my book there.

The final nudge, or perhaps I should call it a hefty shove, was when I had an aura photo taken by the lovely Kevin Doe, a very knowledgeable man. He gave me a reading with it and said, 'You're going to write a book.' I rather rudely said 'Oh that old chestnut.... I don't think so'. But he told me that I would channel it from a Lebanese Cedar Tree. Suddenly, I felt calm, inspired and knew it would then happen!

Here is the proof.

INTRODUCTION

We are often told to go outside and connect more with nature, but many of us don't know how or why.

My aim for this book is to shed more light on the ecological heroism of trees. Not only do they stand as silent sentinels of wisdom, but they also serve as essential custodians of our planet. In their majestic silence, trees inhale our carbon dioxide and exhale our life-sustaining oxygen. A benevolent exchange has sustained our shared existence with a delicate balance for a millennium.

Join me on a transformative adventure of "tree-hugging mindful reflection" and spiritual exploration, where we uncover the profound wisdom held within the serene embrace of nature. The natural world awaits just beyond your doorstep, whether nestled in a forest, adorning a city park, or gracing your own backyard.

The prospect of stepping outside our comfort zone may seem daunting, but this book helps encourage us to silence the noise of modern life and embrace change. By disconnecting from distractions and embracing stillness, we open ourselves to a newfound sense of peace and connection.

As you venture into the great outdoors, you'll not only nourish your body but also nourish your soul. Explore the foraging section to discover the bounty of nature's offerings, from vitamin-rich nuts and berries to pinecones, nature's very own firelighters.

Remember, this journey is a process, and every step you take will bring you closer to a deeper connection with nature and yourself. So, take the first step today with "seeds of hope" and allow the tranquillity of the natural world to guide you on to your own a path of calmness and connection.

1
'Where to Begin' Said The Trees

We have so much wisdom and knowledge to give you – where should we start first?

We have witnessed so much even before human life began. My fellow forefathers saw how the planet evolved and what was needed to sustain life. We are connected through our mycelium network which you humans are slowly beginning to learn and understand. We want to share with you what you can learn from us to strengthen your connections.

We in the forests worldwide all talk and our common observation is how disconnected you all are.

Our hope is that by sharing and laying out the seeds to grow and nourish yourselves, you will be able to follow us. You talk often about connecting with nature, but even those who try still have so much to learn. Let us begin by showing you a different way of growing.

You all understand about being rooted in some way or another, yet you can learn so much from us. We started as seeds, falling a short distance from our mothers. As the damp soil penetrated our shells, they softened, and our biology took over. We knew exactly who we were meant to be! Our roots began to connect with the ground and our brethren. The sun and the rain gave us the energy to keep growing. As our leaves fall, they return to the Earth, a perpetual cycle of birth, death and resurrection begins. We all support each other if we fall ill, or a threat is detected.

Rarely do we see your race doing that consistently.

You often turn to us after a period of illness when you are forced to stop your relentless striving. Striving ... for what??? Money/approval/maybe from someone who doesn't really care about you? discovering that you been living a lie? So, you become ever busier until your body or mind breaks. Only then do you spend "time out in nature". You begin to love it and feel nurtured by us.

We are thrilled to see you, but as you become stronger and start to heal, many of you return to your old ways appearing to have learnt nothing.

This deeply saddens us.

If we can learn to communicate differently with you, offer you a step-by-step guide and a way to balance your growth with time to nurture and time to rest, we will have done our job well.

So, let's begin...

Putting aside the concerns of "global warming", some seasons are naturally wetter, colder or warmer than others. Adaptability and survival are key. On the following pages we will share with you how to stay connected, respect nature and grow as strong as we are.

Cedar of Lebanon – Message

Humans have respected and worked with me for millennia. They use my wood to make their temples because they recognise that I can give them spiritual strength. Let me help you to become rooted in your own spirituality.

"The Wisdom of Trees" Oracle cards by Jane Struthers

2
DEAREST ONES...

There is so much you have yet to learn about us, this planet, and the degrees of reality you live in.

You are never "stuck" or "trapped" in any situation. Within all of us there is the divine spark of creation. Fear has caused some of you to block this. Fear of just how powerful you could be. Judgement has become a learnt behaviour. What if I chose unwisely? If I make a mistake, my choice may upset someone else. We hear all these thoughts and are saddened that you have become so closed off from your true divine self.

Much of this has been laid down in your ancestral DNA. From either a misinterpreted outcome of another's choice, or by those so fearful and insecure that they plant the seeds of doubt and limit another's potential to feel safer in themselves. We implore you to consider how fantastic life could be if you allowed it. Every experience is simply that, an experience.

Just as we use the sunlight and rain to nurture us, look around you and consciously choose what you will use to nourish you.

How can I do that?
I don't know how to change?
There you go again, overthinking and doubting!

Come join us in nature, walk by a river or the sea, or sit by a pond. Give your worries to the water and allow it to wash them away – you don't even need to get wet!

Learning to be quiet and not over stimulated by TV, social media and games for example, you can begin to reconnect with your true self. Remember yourself as a child, before expectation was placed upon you. You were full of limitless potential, everything was an opportunity, a game to play and learn from.

The forest has all the music you need, the gentle wind high up in the treetops, birdsong, rustle in the undergrowth of smaller animals, and the sound of a squirrel eating high up in the tree and dropping its empty shells.

How often have you walked in the woods and never heard any of this?

People say that the older generations are in their second childhood. Good, we think; try not to wait that long and reconnect to your inner childlike wonderment for life right now.

Sit next to us, we are here to support you. You will begin to feel and sense our life force energy flowing through us. Doing this gives you a sense of peace far more significant than that all-inclusive holiday in the sun, where you are tempted to consume too much.

It is at moments like this that you can hear yourself again. Remembering the things that give you joy. Reading a book, and yet you only do that when you're on holiday, once or twice a year, because you perceive yourself as too busy.

You may look at how you spend your days and nights and ask yourself whether the TV programme you love to watch inspires you or feeds your learnt behaviour and need for drama. Addictions come in many shapes and forms; they all serve to distract.

This is the beginning of learning to apply discernment to your life and consciously choose how you live. What if you read a book instead of watching a violent film? You may sleep easier that evening without assistance from pills or drinks. As you become more aware and, in turn, start to make a few small changes, you will create a new growing environment for yourself to flourish in and feel self-nurtured from within.

These are the beginning steps to discovering a fantastic way of living on earth, the more you feel an inner peacefulness, the more you show this to the outer world, and the more those around you sense and feel it. It changes them for the better, so the feeling grows and spreads around your home, workplace, town, neighbouring towns, country, and globe.

"Shinrin Yoku"

The Japanese practice of *forest bathing*.

In simple terms, it is wandering in your local woods and being focused on the natural world around you.

Listen to the birdsong and watch the sunlight dancing on the leaves.

3
The Ancients

After hundreds of years in silence we will be delighted to connect with you again. Over the centuries, we have lived and communed alongside humans. Gradually over time, your lives have become busier and busier, and this coincides with the growth of your intellect and technology. Don't get us wrong; we're not saying that's a bad thing. We hope you will learn to stop judging; nothing is actually good or bad, not even humans.

The ancient ones amongst us miss our contact with you, as Adrienne discovered for herself. On a trip to Southwest Scotland, she visited an ancient wood and heard the call from a Beech Tree. She was with others and felt she couldn't stop. But she knew she should have.

Upon returning to Scotland, she made a beeline for the same woods and found the beech tree, which spoke to her in her mind and invited her to sit, which she did, nestled up against the ancient trunk amongst the leaf mould.

'Thank you for noticing me, said the Beech.' So many these days simply rush by and don't stop.

That simple action has rekindled a lifelong connection across distance and time. Showing you how you can go beyond physical touch connections and the limitations of your beliefs of space and time.

'Have you ever wondered how we feel about being cut down?'

Well, for the most part, it's ok; many of us agree at the beginning of our lives to support you with timbers for your homes, build ships, or heat your homes. To be able to create a tree house platform when we are large enough gives us great joy as your children learn to climb and play in our arms. Not to mention the opportunity for them to "see the world" differently from a greater height. We all hope that the change in perspective will stay with them forever and that they use it throughout their lives when faced with tough challenges or decisions.

We struggle when we do not understand why you might choose to cut us down. Perhaps you feel we are in the wrong place, that is your judgement, not ours. If you are ever faced with the desire or need to fell a tree, please speak to it first. It doesn't matter if you feel silly or doubt it will understand. That's your human conditioning. Speak as you would to an old friend, maybe place a hand on the bark or hug it. Maybe offer to plant another tree to replace it; this would be warmly received. Whether in your garden or even look for a reforesting area that allow you to plant your replacement tree.

A final note on this subject, think, 'What will I do with the wood once the tree has been cut?' Depending on the size and age of the tree, could it be turned into a garden bench become a carved animal or bird, make the stump beautiful, you could even make a walking stick or a Harry Potter wand with the smaller pieces.

Taking on nutrients, you might think the more, the merrier. Perhaps in your fast-paced world you might be tempted to take extra vitamins to make up for missed meals. So, let me tell you a story about a well-meaning human.

They created a new orchard and were so excited when the plum tree blossomed for the very first time. They started thinking about what they would do when the fruit was ready to be harvested. They collected recipes for plum jam, pies and cakes. Then, as spring turned to summer, they were concerned that the trees may not have enough water, so they turned on the hosepipe. Then they became so distracted by their busy life that they forgot to turn it off. What happened? The tree greedily drank, but her shoots could not cope with so much liquid and the stems holding the fruit burst. The well-meaning watering caused the plums to all fall to the ground, and the humans had to wait another year for their first delicious crop.

So, what can you learn from this?

- Don't overwater trees and plants (nature knows best).
- Newly planted trees and plants may need extra water, but once they are established, try not to be in too much of a hurry to force the growth along.
- This applies to humans too; it is best to sip water throughout the day. Your body's cells can then hold onto it and make the best use of it.
- Everything has a time and a season. Some years apples will do well, another year it will be plums. This is why crops are seasonal.

'Trust and flow dearest humans and let go of control.'

Did you know that the world's oldest trees have been around since The Pyramids were built?

And that The Pyramids are believed to have been built between 2550 to 2490BC.

4

All is Not Lost With The Changes in Your World

We have stood for thousands of years, witnessing many comings and goings, we come to you now to share and offer wisdom from all of your trees.

Seasons come and go just like the years – foundations are your key!

Finding the right surroundings to put down roots is so important. We cannot move by ourselves, so if our seeds fall on stony ground or poor soil, they will still grow, but it will take longer, and we will be slower to flourish. As humans, you have the gift of free movement, yet you have forgotten to remain rooted.

If circumstances do not suit your growth, move gently away and begin again. Ensure that you choose the conditions you pick next wisely. Take time to nourish, send your roots down before growing your branches. There is more to growth than just placing your feet upon our earth.

Re-learn to trust your instincts – they will serve you well.

Very few trees stand alone. We entwine our roots and support ourselves and each other above ground. If a tree in a storm partially falls, we can lean on one another and continue to grow. If we collapse completely, with a few roots remaining attached to our earth, we will continue to grow, first horizontally on the forest floor, and then we begin to grow vertically again.

Humans can now communicate virtually using technology, yet you, as a race, have become lonelier and more introspective.

From the beginning of time, your ancestors knew how to communicate, for example using telepathy and scrying with crystals.

You should trust your intuition and learn to stay connected.

Did you know we have an oak tree in Sherwood Forest
that is approximately 1,000 years old.

5
LEAN ON ME

Dearest ones.

As we have said before, we are all here for you to lean on in times of need.

We understand your human existence is multi-faceted. In times of stress, it is easy to become ungrounded. You rely on your mind and learnt behaviours instead of your heart to navigate the situation. Stepping off the hamster wheel and standing on the earth or leaning against one of my brethren will give you so much more clarity.

We see the health worries that so many of you have. Once again, we ask you to look in nature for guidance.

During a strong Winter storm we may lose a branch, even sever one or become uprooted; but watch in the following Spring as we continue to grow despite losing that limb.

We are sure you have come across or seen pictures of a tree blown over in a storm. They still have a few strong roots attached to the earth which continue to grow horizontally rather than vertically.

What can you learn from us?

You can learn perseverance, determination and resilience.

Keep your desire to live your best life, no matter what challenges or obstacles appear to come your way.

Learning and adapting from the trees could bring untold joy your way.

The world's tallest tree is a *Coast Redwood* in California.

It stands 115 metres taller than Big Ben.

6

DISCERN THE TRUTH

Dearest ones, you are blessed and cursed with so much information in your world.

How do you know if what you are being told or shown is true?

Perhaps you never question the information or its sources?

Pure trust is a beautiful thing to behold.

We urge you to learn to discern this information before allowing it to become a fundamental part of your belief system.

Ask yourself "where does it originate from"?

Could it be spiritual guides, the media, friends or other sources of authority?

Are you being led down a false path, particularly one which leads to fear?

One person's truth may well appear false to another. Remember, it is not about being right or wrong.

Try to avoid jumping to conclusions. Give yourself time to go within and ask yourself.

- Does this feel true to me?
- Does it sit well with my inner values and ethics?
- If I change my actions, will someone profit from it? Will there be a higher consciousness benefit?
- Am I being asked to subscribe to a fear-based or heart-centred, love-based topic?

Acknowledge all information without committing to it.

Take time in solitude to go deep within yourself and check how it makes you feel, before pinning your colours and vibration to the mast of yet another crusade.

Hawthorn - Message

Treat me with caution and give me respect because I am an ancient and powerful tree.

My thorns are sharp to give me protection and wherever I grow is said to mark the entrance to the underground realm of the fairies.

"The Wisdom of Trees" Oracle cards by Jane Struthers

7
FORGIVENESS

Dearest ones, we see time differently to you.

Our hearts jump for joy, and our sap rises more quickly when you come to visit us.

Whether you sit in silence and breathe more deeply, or whether you begin to tell us what troubles you. Maybe your work, family, health, or your concerns regarding our beautiful planet.

All of this we rejoice in, and whilst we miss our contact with you, if you have been unable to visit for a while, there is no need to ask for forgiveness – just remember to "be" more in the moment. Let's use just this moment to remind you to step outside of your physical reality. You do not have to wait for the weekend, for suitable weather or when your work pattern allows you time.

Sit quietly wherever you are and take your focus into your heart. Place your hand there and close your eyes. Breathe slowly for a few minutes and set your intention to speak with us. It may be easier to do this if you visualise your favourite tree. Feel her vibration and connect energetically; distance plays no part in this connection.

We all have roots in the same earth and breathe the same air.

Intention is all you need to connect and know you are never alone. We stand here waiting to support you.

Another ancient tree to look out for is:
The Crowhurst Yew in Surrey,
who is approximately 4,000 years old.

See if you can reach your arms around her mighty trunk.

8
How to Connect

You may find yourself fascinated by the shape or colour of a tree, and you make the time to go over and say hi. Touch our bark, pause, close your eyes and breathe. With practice, you will sense the flow of water in our trunk and limbs – our life force. You might like to sit next to us and rest your trunk against ours. If a thought or voice comes into your head or you feel an emotion in your heart, do not "doubt it". You have your first communication!

We are not so different to a new human friend; take time to get to know us. Gain confidence that you can hear or feel our replies. Once this is established, as with any special friendship, you can confide your worries and joys to us. You know, the ones you fear others will laugh about if you tell them ... just talk to us trees!

You can then start asking questions. Not what are the winning Lottery numbers. More about how to move forward in your life, for we have lived many lifetimes and witnessed so much. Many things boil down to the same thing, love or fear.

We invite you to sit quietly in contemplation and open your heart centre.

See your seed, your divine spark in the centre of your heart pulsating brightly with a dazzling gold colour.

Feel its radiance warming your whole human body and spreading out to create an all-encompassing glow around you. Send golden roots down to Mother Earth.

Feel her support and you becoming stronger. Remember, you are never alone. As you spread your roots out, they connect to our mycelium network. One way to communicate with us is to request a tree you have already met, maybe whilst on holiday, to join you. Or if you have a question or concern, ask for a willing tree to step forward.

Make time to grow the connection, ask simple questions and ensure you understand the reply. It may be as a thought entering your mind, a feeling or it may even come to you later in the form of a dream.

You could ask, 'What do you need me to do?'

This connection works both ways. You may learn of a tree or woodland local to you that needs your support in some way.

Look out for the calling to visit a particular tree in person.

Hazel – Message

My history of being planted in hedgerows mean I am an ancient guardian of boundaries, both physical and spiritual. Let me teach you how to set your own boundaries so you know where to concentrate your power and wisdom.

"The Wisdom of Trees" Oracle cards by Jane Struthers

9
Listening and Asking Questions

Yes, dearest Lebanese Cedar tree, I got the message from your forest brethren to move my Bistro table and chairs from the patio to under my wonderful Walnut tree. So why am I not there now? Well, it's raining, and humans are less waterproof than trees, especially when I am sitting down writing this very book in my lovely cork covered journal.

Watch Out!

For what? As a race, you need to become more adaptable; many of you are trying, but more need to step up.

Question 'Ok, how do we reach them'? I asked.

Answer 'By your actions; more will follow once they understand how'.

Question 'What is a tree's job or role'?

Answer' To live and store information, which we hold in our trunks'. The growth rings you see when a tree has been felled show climate information, slow tight rings, hot seasons, lack of water, thicker rings plentiful supply. We observe that many humans need to connect to the bigger picture. You tend to look just in front of your feet with little or no idea of what is going on around you or the impact that your actions or lack of actions may have. As our planet upgrades energetically and spiritually, the human aura (your energy fields) has grown beyond the original six feet circumference to a now staggering twenty miles. We eagerly wait to witness your abilities to stay connected with this bigger reality.

We also create a home for other animals and insects to live in and be supported by. For example, did you know a mature oak tree can hold 2,300 species of birds, bryophytes (moss, liverworts), fungi, invertebrates, lichen and mammals?

Also, we need to reproduce with our multiple different seeds, some carried by the wind, some by birds, and others fall to the ground to germinate where they fall. Or are eaten by animals and passed through their gut to colonise a new area. So, you can see, dearest humans, whilst you have legs and we a trunk, there are so many similarities between our species:

- To Survive
- To learn and hold information
- To create a home
- To reproduce.

So, is it any wonder that many of you feel connected when you spend time alone with us?

If you can only learn to broaden your horizons and see where you fit into this world, you will never feel that sense of being lost or alone.

Question 'So, what action do I need to take'?

Answer Try to be in harmony with nature, the seasons, and the space around you. You almost need to detox, in your words, to support this. You cannot listen when busy, or your mind is not still. Remember, this will impact down as far as the cells in your body.

Take conscious decisions to slow down whenever possible. Be aware of the food and drink you consume, "a little of what you fancy does you good". Water may be boring to some, but all life is based on it. If trees have no water, they drop their leaves early in an attempt to prolong life; the alternative is they will die. So, you see, water is valuable, so you need to hydrate your body and mind. Now you will gain clarification on signs of hunger, which means, more often than not, you're simply thirsty. Any potential addiction to sweet sugary rushes will reduce until your awareness spots the triggers and results.. Your mind will become ever so slightly clearer, so when you now try to still it, you can. Meditation will become more achievable, and it is from this place of calmness that our messages can start to be seen or heard.

Silver Birch – Message

I am the mother of the forest.

My trunk and branches look delicate, but I am strong because I bend with the wind.

If you work with me, I will teach you how to cleanse your body and your spirit to find peace and complete health.

"The Wisdom of Trees" Oracle cards by Jane Struthers

10

Five Seasons of Our Life

In this next section you will learn how to see and feel the changes that happen during each season.

Energetically there are not four, but five seasons. By understanding these, you will be able to structure your own lives to the natural rhythms of nature which are all around us.

You can learn to live with nature, take your cues from us and the flora that grow alongside us.

Learn to adopt this approach as much as possible and you may be able to find your mental health and energy levels improve and that they are more sustainable.

Within these sections you will see reference to foraging and what to look for, please remember these guidelines.

Guidelines for Foraging

- Know what you are picking, if in doubt leave it
- Seek permission from the site owner (private land) and from the plant or tree and give gratitude
- Only take what you will use, leaving plenty behind for others to enjoy – it's easy to get carried away
- Do not collect rare species.

Why forage you may ask? Well, there is a wonderful abundance of fruit and nuts available during the year, packed full of goodness, it is what your ancestors always did.

You can also decorate your home with different foliage, flowers and nuts, bringing nature's beauty inside. There are so many benefits for example, did you know you can even use Chestnuts to help repel spiders?

Spring

March, April and May

The element of this season is Wood - Keynote is Mental Activity

Spring Equinox, when the daylight once again equals the length of darkness beckons my fellow trees to allow their leaf buds to swell, as our sap starts to rise. Pussy willow and catkins begin to dance in the early sunshine, heralding the return of more sunshine to our world.

We are hopeful each Spring as our energy awakens us from our Winter rest. We also hope for humankind to awaken. For many tens of thousands of years, we hoped in vain.

However, more and more of you are beginning to view your world differently.

So, each Spring, consider what you truly hope for. Set the seeds of hope to bring your dreams to life.

The more you can tune into the rhythm of nature and her seasons, the more your hope is fulfilled.

March - This is a time to become more mentally active, rather than physically active. Allow your excitement to build and plan how you want to move forward. In other words, start to set your seeds both physically and metaphorically.

- Foraging - Look for gorse flowers, early nettles, velvet shank mushrooms.

April - in March you rise from your Winter slumber, you can start to allow your energy to flow. Create time to go for longer walks in nature or a local wood. Start to look in your gardens and see what action is needed. The magnolia trees begin to blossom, although a sudden frost can still catch them out and damage their beautiful blooms.

Remember to keep working towards your bigger life plans.

- Foraging - Look for more wild plants, wild garlic, hairy bittercress, young bramble leaves and nettles.

May - The warmer days are now returning with some earnest, and you see the trees becoming fully covered with leaves of amazing shades of green. Orchards begin to fill with apple blossom, bluebells cover the woodland floor, and the bees are busy pollinating.

Make time to embrace this increased creative energy, which of your plans will you realise first?

- Foraging - Look for small, young lime tree leaves, hawthorn flowers, red clover and chickweed.

Points to remember:

- Make notes of where you have seen certain trees or plants so you can revisit at different times of the year.
- Start collecting recipes to use your foraged items and not waste them.
- Note how you feel in certain locations, calm or energised

SUMMER
JUNE AND JULY

The element of this season is Fire - Keynote is Intuition, Joy and Peace

Life is flowing freely and at a fast pace. Bask in the sunlight, for that is the life force we all grow from. Step out of your home or office and put down your devices. Pause and be fully present with us, if only for ten minutes. Breathe more deeply and feel that connection.

Are your spring seeds still growing?

Did you remember to tend them?

Try not to be harsh on yourself. There is always time. Simply pick up where you left off.

In Summer we celebrate the Summer Solstice, the longest day of light each year.

June - "Flaming June" as you often call it. The summer heat returns and everything in nature grows very quickly. Prepare yourself to take more action; maybe increase your exercise. Walking is a very gentle yet powerful thing to do and takes you out into our natural world, where you can connect to nature's inspiration.

- Foraging - Look for ash seeds (keys), elder flowers, lime flowers, dog rose petals and honeysuckle flowers.

July - Continue to be busy getting ever closer to your goals and dreams. Remember to connect to your inner sense of peace and joy during these long, warm sunny days but take nothing for granted.

- Foraging - Look for bilberry, chanterelle mushrooms and wild strawberries.

Points to remember:

- Make notes of where you have seen certain trees or plants so you can revisit at different times of the year.
- Start collecting recipes to use your foraged items and not waste them.
- Note how you feel in certain locations, calm or energised.

Late Summer

August

The Element of this season is Earth - Keynote is Pondering.

Everything in nature is full of high energy, flowering and growing fast, but a word of warning dear ones. It is very easy to over expend your energy at this time, so try to slow down. We see you enjoying the late summer evenings relaxing with family and friends over a drink. This is wonderful. It gives you the opportunity to reconnect with the Earth and yourselves, the dreams and desires you started with this year. See how they too are flourishing and enjoy that sense of achievement.

August - A time to pause and enjoy the flowers in your gardens and the flowering of your goals and dreams. Allow yourselves to ponder on life and ask yourself is it going the way I wanted? Remember you can change direction at any time.

- Foraging - Look for the first signs of hazelnuts, rowan berries, blackberries, elderberries, and crab apples.

Points to remember:

- Make notes of where you have seen certain trees or plants, so you can revisit at different times of the year.
- Start collecting recipes to use your foraged items and not waste them.
- Note how you feel in certain locations, calm or energised.

AUTUMN
SEPTEMBER, OCTOBER AND NOVEMBER

The Element of this season is Metal - Keynote is Orderliness and Rightness.

The Autumn Equinox is when the day and night are of equal length and from this point on, we begin to receive more darkness and less daylight. In fact, this once marked the beginning of the New Year, rather than the usual 1st January celebration. Some of my fellow trees allow their leaves to change colour and after a brief time of splendour they let them fall to the ground. As they begin to decay and return to Mother Earth animals may use them for winter bedding. Our life force sap begins to slow down.

September - as you sat back and enjoyed last month, what insights came to you? Now is a time to get your lives and dreams in order. Let go of anything that no longer serves you or didn't come to full fruition. Nature shows you its abundance as all trees and plants are heavily laden with their produce.

- Foraging - look out for beech nuts, rosehips, hawthorn berries, sloes, wild strawberries and raspberries.

October - The heat of the sunlight is beginning to lose some of its fire. This is time to begin to harvest from nature and enjoy the fruits of your labours.

- Foraging - Look for bullace (a form of wild plum), beech nuts, hazel nuts, rose hip, sloes, sweet chestnuts and walnuts.

November - A time of reducing sunlight when the temperature begins to fall. All of nature slows down after the busy Autumn harvesting.

So, ask yourself - how can I apply this to my life?
Consider where will you get your energy and fuel from this Winter?

As humans you cannot go into a full state of dormant hibernation as we can, although those of you who suffer from depression may be in a similar state and withdraw from your physical world. Think about what you can do to change your habits, and mirror more clearly what nature is showing you.

As our leaves drop, we need less nourishment, so perhaps use this sign from us to make your own changes and flow more with nature. Some of your human activities remain the same all year round for example earning your livings. However, look at your waking hours and consider where you could choose to slow down.

- Foraging - Look for the last of the bullace, pine nuts/needles and sweet chestnuts.

Extra

If you find this period too dark, take time out and consider your future dreams and aspirations. Booking a holiday may well only serve as a short term distraction or rest bite from reality.

Rather ask yourself - what would really light you up inside?

Dream big when you answer this, then simply plot out the steps to make it happen.

Points to remember:

- Make notes of where you have seen certain trees or plants, so you can revisit at different times of the year.
- Start collecting recipes to use your foraged items and not waste them.
- Note how you feel in certain locations, calm or energised.

WINTER
DECEMBER, JANUARY AND FEBRUARY

The element of this season is Water - Keynote is Will Power.

High winds, frost and snow can cause us to let go of our branches. Often these are weakened through illness, or perhaps we grew too quickly in the Spring and we were not able to support this new growth.

When we are covered with a deep layer of frost or snow, we go deeper within ourselves. We expend less energy to survive and yet we are still very much alive. You may not see this but you will feel it if you touch our bark.

The Winter Solstice is celebrated, and we enter the darkest period on Earth, with far less daylight. Our message to you is to 'go within and reflect'. What do you need to let go of? Holding on for too long will only cause you more difficulty and possibly damage.

The month of December can be challenging for humans, with so many expectations for your holiday season. We implore you to remember to look outside at nature, take your lead from what is going on around you. The darker nights show you it is time to rest more and save your energy wherever possible. Set a strong intention that this year December will be different. You will not overspend your energy or your finances, remember it's all energy just in different forms.

We see the amount of gifts being bought that are often not appreciate or required, maybe it's the perfect time of year to set a limit on the amount you spend?

Are the presents you give sustainable for the planet?

Wrapping paper can cause a trail of destruction if it cannot biodegrade easily.

Use your will power wisely and you will reap the benefits later, especially when the bills come in next month.

December - Notice what is happening in nature and try to apply it to your life. You are entering a period to rest within and the opportunity to recharge your energy. However, this will only be achieved if you create space and time for yourself, even fifteen minutes every day will make a difference to how you feel.

- Foraging - Look for any remaining sweet chestnuts and pine nuts/needles.

January - Resting more deeply is the key. Ask yourself what is happening to your life force energy?
Are you still overusing it by worrying about things you cannot change?
Are you still living your life at the fast pace of Summer?
Perhaps it is time for you to ask for help?

In January Winter is fully upon us, snow may lay on our branches, but our life force energy is still there, and our sap flows deep within our trunks.
Ask yourself what runs deep within you?
January could be a time of learning. Reflect on your past experiences and may be gain inspiration and move forward and grow during the next season.

- Foraging - Look for any remaining acorns, beech nuts, hazel nuts and chestnuts. Most berries will long ago have been eaten.

February - Hints of Spring begin to show with early flowering bulbs. Watch the wise trees, who do not rush into leaf too early. They know that a sudden frost could damage them. Be guided by their wisdom, do not rush too quickly to put your new plans into action. Expending too much energy too quickly may mean your dreams could stall. You may not be able to sustain the increased demands on your energy.

Use your willpower and hold your resolve to rest as much as possible during this last month of Winter. The nights may be showing signs of reducing and the daylight gradually lengthening, but you need patience while this happens.

- Foraging - There is less to find, mainly a few wild plants.

Points to remember:

- Make notes of where you have seen certain trees or plants, so you can revisit at different times of the year.
- Start collecting recipes to use your foraged items and not waste them.
- Note how you feel in certain locations, calm or energised.

SUMMARY

My earnest desire in creating this book is to ignite a spark within you.

I hope that you use this book as your gateway to a profound journey of self-discovery and interconnectedness.

Beyond the tangible, lies a deeper connection that unites us all in ways we may not fully grasp.

I encourage you to go outside, each time you will uncover more of the joy and solace just waiting there for you.

For those eager to delve deeper into the exploration, I invite you to connect with me and stay tuned for upcoming offerings that I have designed to facilitate and enrich your connection with nature and fellow humans.

With heartfelt gratitude,
Adrienne

Full details of events and opportunities for personal growth are available at:
www.adriennegreen.co.uk

Join me on Facebook and gain free wisdom from: Light up Your life with Adrienne Green.

Acknowledgements

The existence of this book serves as a testament to the notion that our capacity for growth knows no bounds, regardless of age or level of knowledge. All it took is a genuine connection to my passion for an idea or project, coupled with nurturing and allowing it to flourish. In this journey, I have encountered the invaluable support and guidance of knowledgeable individuals who come forward at the right moment.

With heartfelt appreciation, I extend my deepest gratitude to the following individuals, whose contributions have made the realization of this book possible. Without their assistance, this work would not have come to fruition, and you would not be holding it in your hands today.

Anna-Louise Haigh an amazingly gifted guide, teacher and soul whisperer, who truly started my awakening.
www.anna-louisehaigh.com

Patrick Gamble, whose dedication to giving daily support, inspiration and guidance, inspires so many. Not to mention being a truly gifted spiritual artist. **www.patrickgamble.co.uk**

Kevin Doe, my amazing aura guy, check out if he is coming to a town near you! **info@aura-interpretations.com**

Lorna Vyse, a dear friend and talented new author, who supports families and young children deal with bereavement and who connected me with "Write That Book". **www.lornavyse.com**

Michael Heppell, a Sunday Times No1 best-selling author, international speaker and coach, who created the "Write That Book" (WTB) programme (now available as a book), to enable other budding authors to achieve their dreams. **www.michaelheppell.com**

The very patient Jenn Garside, illustrator and graphic designer, who created this amazing cover for my book. **Jenn.garside.illustrations@gmail.com**

Matthew J Bird, who took away all the worries of typesetting and formatting and made the book publication ready. **www.JackFruitTreasure.com**

My fellow alchemists support group from WTB, Desiree De Beer, Gail Molyneaux, Jane Brady, Kay Dobson-Bennet, Sonja Batt and special thanks to Carolyn Parry, who never once stopped encouraging us all through the blood, sweat and tears and led by shining example being the first across the line with her fabulous book – "Change Your Story". **www.careeralchemy.co.uk**

And finally (but by no means least) Kyra Cruise, my editor, proofreader, fellow author and Wellbeing Advocate. **kyracruise7@gmail.com**

About The Author

I had a relatively conventional upbringing. I was an only child born in Plymouth, Devon, and yet I was fortunate enough to live in Singapore for my early years. We moved around a lot with my father's work. I would always have a small piece of my parents' garden to call my own, and I loved tending to the plants and flowers. Of course, I can now see how the young me was grounding herself in nature!

So, my love of nature was there from an early age – even though I didn't like dirty hands and would always to the amusement and delight of my family say, 'wash hands, mummy'. To this day, you will always find me wearing gardening gloves, even though I am big enough to wash my own hands now.

I finally put down my roots in Norfolk on the east coast of England, where I have lived for nearly 30 years.

Having had a successful career in finance, my mid-life crisis or awakening, depending on your viewpoint, arrived around 2000. It was time for a complete change as I began to discover my true calling. This led me to create a successful career, this time in the holistic world, which saw me teaching around the UK and internationally.

I am passionate about using my "holistic tool kit" empowering people to listen to their own intuition and create their life to their highest potential. I use Soul Centred

Crystal Healing, Reflexology, The Balance Procedure, Angelic Reiki and I am a Holy Fire® Reiki Master Teacher and other deeper spiritual work. I also found time to run life-changing retreats in Glastonbury and Norfolk.

As I continue to evolve, I am led by the strong call of nature. Her rhythms run within me and lead me to want to teach people how to meditate and connect with nature, the moon cycles and, of course, the ancient wisdom of the trees.

And now I find myself being guided to write this, my first book, which I hope you will enjoy as a guide, an inspiration and a handy tool. Please feel free to share this far and wide, for the more we learn and connect the more we all grow. Just like the trees!

Full details of events and opportunities for personal growth are available at: **www.adriennegreen.co.uk**

Join me on Facebook and gain free wisdom: Light Up Your life with Adrienne Green.